NORFOLK
COUNTRY RECIPES

COMPILED BY
MOLLY PERHAM

RAVETTE BOOKS

Published by Ravette Books Limited
3 Glenside Estate, Star Road,
Partridge Green, Horsham,
Sussex RH13 8RA
(0403) 710392

Production: Oval Projects Ltd.
Cover design: Jim Wire
Typesetting: Repro-type
Printing & binding: Nørhaven A/S

All recipes are given in Imperial and Metric
weights and measures. Where measurements
are given in 'cups', these are American cups,
holding 8 fluid ounces.

The recipes contained in this book are traditional
and many have been compiled from archival sources.
Every effort has been made to ensure that the recipes
are correct.

RECIPES

SOUPS and BEGINNINGS

FISH

POULTRY and GAME

MEAT

SUNDRIES

CAKES and BISCUITS

NORFOLK

The flatness of Norfolk makes it ideal agricultural land. Wide vistas of wheat, barley and rye — broken by an old windmill or two — are a familiar sight. The Norfolk Dumpling is testimony to this grain-producing heritage — eaten in the traditional way with the gravy before the main meal, it took the edge off the appetite. When times were hard it replaced the meat. Savoury suet crust puddings are another Norfolk speciality.

Familiar, too, in June, are the brilliant yellow fields of mustard in flower. Jeremiah Colman opened his first mustard mill near Norwich in 1814, and mustard seed has been produced in the area ever since.

Soft fruit and vegetables thrive in the rich soil. Raspberries, strawberries, red and black currants are made into puddings, preserves and jam. Asparagus and peas are cultivated on a large scale. East Anglia is the only place in the country where wild samphire — an edible dark green fleshy marsh plant rather like the asparagus — is harvested and sold.

Norfolk turkeys were once famous worldwide. An annual turkey fair was held at Attleborough. Turkeys used to be driven to London on foot for Christmas — a journey that took three months. Daniel Defoe recorded in the early 18th century that each year 300 droves of Norfolk turkeys went through the town of Stratford St. Mary in Suffolk, on their way to London. The county is still an important turkey-rearing centre.

Young swans, too, used to be a local delicacy, and could still be obtained right up until the 1930s. In 1931 an advertisement appeared in the Personal columns of *The Times* for 'Cygnets supplied dressed for dinner and banquets' — Master, Great Hospital, Norwich.

Norfolk sheep graze on marshes at the edge of the sea — local lamb and mutton is considered to be of superior quality, not least by King Edward VII, who acquired a taste for it at Sandringham. Beef recipes are scarce as this is not a beef-producing country, but there are many tasty ways of preparing the cottagers' pig.

The fields of grain, coastal marshes and inland lakes of the Broads provide shelter for all kinds of game birds — partridge, pheasant, quail and wild ducks. When meat was scarce these provided the Norfolk countryman with something for the pot, and also provided sport for the shooting parties that were held on the country estates. Before the improvement of agriculture the county was overrun with rabbits, and these formed a major part of the farmworkers' diet. They were known as 'hollow meat' — and it was a common practice when a man was hired by a farm to make a proviso that he should be fed 'hollow meat' only a certain number of days a week.

In the past, Norfolk's long coastline has provided a livelihood for many fishermen. For many years the city of Norwich had to deliver 24 herring pies each year to Court. This feudal custom originated when the valley of the River Yare was still an estuary, and Norwich was an important fishing port. By the 12th century Great Yarmouth had become the centre of the herring industry, with numerous smokehouses to produce local bloaters, kippers and buckling. Herring and boiled potatoes used to be the staple diet of a substantial section of the population. Cod is also plentiful, and all kinds of shellfish — mussels, cockles, whelks, shrimps, and the famous Cromer crab.

Today there is a revival of interest in foods such as the crab, smoked fish, samphire and dumplings, and visitors to Norfolk will be able to enjoy these and other local delicacies.

'Yarmouth has first (O more than happy Port)
The honour to receive the King and Court
And entertain, season providing dishes
The King of England with the King of Fishes.'

Matthew Stevenson, on the occasion of King
Charles II's visit to Yarmouth in 1761

PEA SOUP WITH NORFOLK DUMPLINGS

Serves 4

12 oz (350 g) split peas
1 smoked hock
2 pints (1.15 litres/ 5 cups) water
1 onion
3 carrots
3 sticks celery

Soak the split peas in cold water overnight.

Put the smoked hock in a saucepan with the water.

Bring to the boil and simmer for 1 hour.

Remove the hock and add the soaked split peas to the water.

Bring back to the boil and skim the top.

Add the chopped onion, carrots and celery.

Remove the skins from the hock, cut the meat from the bone and add it to the saucepan.

Simmer the soup for 1-1½ hours, adding the Norfolk Dumplings (see recipe) about 20 minutes before the end.

Peas.

NORFOLK DUMPLINGS

There are basically two ways of making Norfolk dumplings: baking in the oven alongside the roast meat, or boiling with a stew or soup. The baked dumplings were traditionally eaten with gravy before the meat as a filler-up — rather like Yorkshire pudding in the North. Boiled dumplings were cooked in plain boiling water and served as a dessert with jam, treacle, or butter and sugar.

Baked dumplings:
8 oz (225 g) self-raising flour
A pinch of salt
6 oz (175 g) shredded suet
Milk

Grease an ovenproof dish.

Mix together the flour, salt and shredded suet with enough milk to make a soft dough.

Knead into a flat round and place in the ovenproof dish.

Mark criss-cross lines on the top and brush with milk to glaze.

Bake alongside the meat for 30-40 minutes.

Serve in the traditional way with gravy, as a first course, or with the meat.

Oven: 375°F/190°C Gas Mark 5

Boiled dumplings:
1 lb (450 g) plain flour
A pinch of salt
½ oz (15 g) lard
½ oz (15 g) fresh yeast
1 level teaspoon sugar
Warm water

Sift the flour and salt into a mixing basin.

Rub in the lard.

Cream the yeast with the sugar and a little warm water.

Pour this into the flour and add enough warm water to make an elastic dough.

Knead well until the dough is smooth.

Cover the dough with a cloth and leave in a warm place until it has doubled in size.

Knead again and divide into equal portions.

Shape into small balls and leave to rise for a further 10-15 minutes.

Add to a broth or stew for the last 20 minutes of cooking time, or if eating as a dessert, cook for 20 minutes in gently boiling salted water.

SPOON DUMPLINGS

2 eggs
¼ pint (150 ml/ ⅔ cup) milk
A pinch of salt
Self-raising flour

Whisk the eggs and stir in the milk.

Add a pinch of salt.

Gradually add enough flour to make a thick batter.

Bring to the boil a saucepan of water.

Drop spoonsful of the batter into the boiling water and cook until set right through — this takes about 4 minutes.

Strain the dumplings and turn them into a warmed serving dish.

Add a knob of butter and a little brown sugar and eat hot.

Alternatively, serve with soup or stew.

Flower Dredger

SHRIMP STARTER

Pink shrimps come from the coast around Yarmouth. The shells come off more easily if they are cooked in unsalted water. The following dish makes a good starter to a meal.

4 oz (100 g) fresh or frozen shrimps, cooked and peeled
White wine
A pinch of nutmeg
Pepper
6 eggs
Milk
A knob of butter

Heat the shrimps gently in a little white wine, and sprinkle with the nutmeg and pepper.

Beat the eggs with a little milk and cook gently in a saucepan until thick and creamy.

Stir the shrimps into the scrambled eggs and add a knob of butter.

Serve with thinly sliced brown bread and butter.

Shrimps

NORFOLK FISH PIE

1 lb (450 g) cod fillet
½ pint (300 ml/ 1¼ cups) cider
1 lb (450 g) potatoes
Salt and pepper
Milk
1 oz (25 g) butter
1 oz (25 g) flour
1 large tomato
2 oz (50 g) grated cheese

Cut the cod into ½ inch (1 cm) cubes.

Put into a saucepan with the cider, bring to the boil, cover and simmer for 15 minutes.

Drain and put into the centre of a serving dish.

Keep the fish warm and reserve the cooking liquid.

Peel and boil the potatoes, and mash with a little milk.

Season with salt and pepper and arrange around the fish.

For the sauce, melt the butter in a saucepan and stir in the flour.

Cook gently for 1 minute, then gradually add the liquid in which the fish was cooked, stirring to prevent lumps forming.

Bring the sauce to the boil, season with salt and pepper and pour over the fish.

Arrange slices of tomato on top and sprinkle with the cheese.

Brown under a hot grill.

COD WITH OYSTER SAUCE

This recipe is also suitable for haddock or hake.

**1 pint (600 ml/ 2½ cups) court bouillon made from fish
trimmings, a carrot, onion and herbs**
A cod weighing about 1-1½ lb (450-675 g)
A glass of white wine
1 onion
½ teaspoon grated nutmeg
A bouquet garni
Salt and pepper
1 oz (25 g) flour
1 oz (25 g) butter
8 oysters

Make the court bouillon by simmering fish bones and
trimmings, a carrot, an onion and herbs in water for 30
minutes.

Place the fish in a saucepan and pour over the court bouillon
and the wine.

Add the finely chopped onion, nutmeg, bouquet garni, and
seasoning.

Simmer gently for about 30 minutes until the flesh flakes
easily.

Put the fish on to a serving dish and keep warm.

Melt the butter in a saucepan and stir in the flour.

Cook for a couple of minutes, then add the strained liquor
from the fish, stirring all the time to prevent lumps.

When the sauce has thickened, add the oysters and pour
over the cod.

Serve hot.

TO MAKE A HERRING-PYE

The fishing ports on the east coast of England were the centre of the herring industry. The Great Yarmouth Herring Fair, which lasted from Michaelmas to Martinmas (29th September - 11th November) was first held in 1270 and went on until well into the 18th century.

Until comparatively recently the Sheriff of Norwich held thirty acres of land by the service of twenty-four herring pies, each containing one hundred and twenty fish. In 1629 the Secretary of State complained of 'the poor quality of the fish' and that the pies were short weight! This recipe is dated 1752.

Take your Herrings split, headed, scalded, boned and washed. Then make a good Puff-paste, and lay your Dish or Pattipan, season your Herrings with spice, and lay a layer of Butter and a layer of Herrings, till all is in. Then take three Anchovies, Eel, cop'd small, hard Yolks of Eggs, Marrow, Sweet Herbes, a few Oisters, some small Pepper, grated Bread and Nutmeg. Make up the Forced-meat with raw Eggs into Balls, some round; lay them about your Herrings; put Butter over all, lid your pye, and an hour will bake it.

HERRINGS IN WINE

4 herrings
1 tablespoon chopped parsley
1 small onion, chopped
2 oz (50 g) butter
A glass of red wine

Clean the fish, remove the heads and make 3 cuts on each side.

Place in an ovenproof dish.

Sprinkle over the chopped parsley and onion.

Dot the top with knobs of butter.

Put into a moderately hot oven until the butter has melted, then pour over the wine and cook for a further 20 minutes, or until the fish is tender.

Oven: 400°F/200°C Gas Mark 6

HERRINGS WITH MUSTARD SAUCE

Serves 4

4 herrings

For the mustard sauce:
1 oz (25 g) flour
A pinch of salt
½ pint (300 ml/ 1¼ cups) milk
1 oz (25 g) sugar
½ oz (15 g) butter
1 teaspoon mustard powder
Vinegar

Clean and gut the herrings.

Bring a large pan of salted water to the boil and put in the herrings.

Boil for 10 minutes.

To make the sauce:

Mix the flour and salt with a little milk to make a paste.

Gradually add the rest of the milk, stirring to prevent lumps.

Put a drop of water in a saucepan and bring to the boil, then add the milk mixture and stir over a low heat until it thickens.

Stir in the sugar and butter, and then the mustard powder mixed with vinegar.

Drain the herrings and serve hot with the mustard sauce.

BOILED HERRINGS

Serves 4

4 herrings
1 tablespoon lemon juice
6 peppercorns
Salt and pepper

Remove the heads, open and clean the herrings, but leave in the roes.

Put the herrings into a large pan and cover with water.

Add the lemon juice, peppercorns, salt and pepper.

Bring slowly to the boil, then simmer for about 10 minutes, or until the herrings are tender.

FRIED HERRINGS

Serves 4

4 herrings, filleted
2 oz (50 g) semolina
Salt and pepper
Fat or oil for frying

Season the semolina with salt and pepper and coat the herrings.

Fry in hot fat or oil for about 15 minutes, turning once.

Serve with mustard sauce.

SOUSED HERRINGS

Serves 4

4 herrings, filleted
1 oz (25 g) flour
Salt and pepper
½ teaspoon powdered mace
1 oz (25 g) butter
A sprig of parsley
1 bay leaf
¼ pint (150 ml/ ⅔ cup) water
¼ pint (150 ml/ ⅔ cup) white wine vinegar

Dust the fillets with flour seasoned with salt, pepper and mace.

Place a knob of butter in the centre of each fillet, sprinkle with chopped parsley and roll up, skin side out.

Put the herrings in an ovenproof dish and add the bay leaf, water and vinegar.

Cover and bake for 1 hour in a moderately hot oven.

Serve cold, with slices of buttered bread.

Oven: 375°F/190°C Gas Mark 5

RED HERRING

This is the oldest form of cured herring, smoked before gutting. They were discovered accidentally — so we are told — by a fisherman who hung his surplus catch from the rafters of his cabin and forgot about them. The smokey fire beneath gradually turned them bright red.

Red herring are first salted and then smoked hard. They used to be popular because they kept well in hot weather without refrigeration. These days they are difficult to find, but if you do manage to get hold of them they can be eaten uncooked in thin slices, with bread and butter.

Alternatively, an old Norfolk method was to soak them in milk before grilling. They were then served with potatoes or eggs.

BUCKLING

Also rare these days, the buckling is a herring that has been hot-smoked — that is, cooked — with its innards intact. It is much softer than the red herring and can be eaten with bread and butter and horseradish sauce.

A good fish paste can be made with skinned and filleted buckling, mixed with butter, lemon and a little garlic.

BUTTERED BLOATERS

Serves 4

Great Yarmouth produced the first mild smoke cure in 1835, and named the product a bloater. A bloater is a whole ungutted herring and is not split open down the back, like a kipper.

4 bloaters
2 oz (50 g) butter
Juice of half a lemon
Salt and pepper

Cut the heads, tails and fins from the bloaters and remove the skin and bones.

Put the bloaters into a buttered, ovenproof dish.

Dot with butter, sprinkle over the lemon juice and season with salt and pepper.

Cover with foil and bake in a moderate oven for 15 minutes.

Serve on hot buttered toast.

Oven: 350°F/180°C Gas Mark 4

BLOATER PASTE

This fish spread is very popular spread on toast for breakfast.

4 bloaters
About 4 oz (100 g) butter
½ tablespoon lemon juice
Pepper

Cook the bloaters in boiling water for 5 minutes.

Remove the flesh from the bones and weigh it — you need half this amount of butter.

Mince the bloater flesh and add the lemon juice.

Pound the minced flesh with the butter to a smooth paste, adding pepper to taste.

Pot the paste in individual dishes and cover with clarified butter.

YARMOUTH STRAWS

8 oz (225 g) shortcrust pastry
2 oz (50 g) grated cheese
Cayenne pepper
8 oz (225 g) kipper fillets

Roll out the pastry on a floured surface to a thickness of ¼ inch (5 mm).

Sprinkle half the grated cheese over the pastry, and a little cayenne pepper.

Fold the pastry into three and roll out again.

Sprinkle over the rest of the cheese and a little cayenne pepper.

Fold into three and roll out again to ⅛ inch (3 mm) thick.

Cut into strips approximately ¼ inch (5 mm) wide by 3 inch (7.5 cm) long.

Cut the kippers into strips the same size.

Put a strip of pastry with a strip of kipper and twist them together.

Place on greased baking sheets and bake in a moderate oven for 20 minutes.

Oven: 375°F/190°C Gas Mark 5

KIPPER SAVOURY

2 large kippers
2 oz (50 g) butter
1 tablespoon chopped chives
A clove of garlic

For the pastry:
8 oz (225 g) plain flour
3 oz (75 g) lard
3 oz (75 g) peeled and grated raw potato
A little water

Simmer the kippers in boiling water until the flesh comes away from the bones easily.

Soften the butter in a basin and add the flaked kipper flesh, chives and crushed garlic.

Sift the flour into a mixing basin and rub in the lard.

Add the potato and enough water to make a firm dough.

Roll out half the dough to line a greased 8 inch (20 cm) pie plate.

Spoon in the kipper filling.

Roll out the other half of the dough to make the lid.

Dampen the edges of the pastry, press them together to seal, trim and flute with a knife.

Make a criss-cross pattern on top of the pie with a sharp knife, cutting through the pastry.

Brush with melted butter.

Bake in a moderately hot oven for 30-40 minutes until golden brown.

Oven: 400°F/200°C Gas Mark 6

DRESSED CRAB

Cromer is famous for its crabs. When you buy a crab at the fishmonger's it will already have been boiled. Choose one that is heavy for its size and looks very fresh. They are at their best from May to October. An average crab measuring about 6 inches (15 cm) across should weigh about 2½-3 lbs (1.25 - 1.5 kg) and is enough for four people.

1 crab, weighing about 2½-3 lbs (1.25 - 1.5 kg)
Salt and pepper
Fresh white breadcrumbs
Lemon juice
French dressing (olive oil and vinegar)
1 hard-boiled egg
Parsley

Pick the crab meat from the shell.

Clean the shell thoroughly.

Mix the dark meat with the breadcrumbs and lemon juice and season with salt and pepper.

Arrange around the edge of the shell.

Mix the white meat with French dressing and pile into the centre of the shell.

Garnish with the sliced hard-boiled egg and chopped parsley.

Buy a Crabb

NORFOLK MUSSEL PUDDING

2 pints (1 litre) mussels
8 oz (225 g) self-raising flour
3 oz (75 g) shredded suet
Salt and pepper

Wash the mussels thoroughly and remove the beards.

Put them in a large pan without a lid.

Cook over a gentle heat until they open.

Remove the shells.

Mix the flour, suet and a pinch of salt together with enough water to make a firm dough.

Roll out three-quarters of the dough to line a greased pudding basin.

Pile the mussels inside, seasoned with salt and pepper.

Roll out the remaining dough to make a lid.

Cover with greaseproof paper and foil, or a pudding cloth.

Steam for 2 hours — or reduce the steaming time by using a pressure cooker.

Mussels

COCKLES AND WHELKS

The coasted area around Wells-next-the-sea is famous for its cockles and whelks. At Brancaster Staithe the boatment go out for miles for the whelk fishing. Whelks are sold ready cooked — they are boiled in big coppers in sheds on the edge of the marshes.

The best cockles come from Stiffkey. They are known as Stewkey Blues because of their blueish shell.

To prepare the cockles:

Wash the cockles well to remove any particles of sand — it is best to let them soak in fresh water for a couple of hours.

Put them into a heavy saucepan without any water, cover, and heat gently.

The cockles will open and are ready to eat.

Serve warm with a knob of butter, or cold with vinegar.

COCKLES AND BACON

Serves 4

This is a favourite way of eating cockles locally.

1 pint (600 ml/ 2½ cups) cockles
8 rashers streaky bacon
Toast

Wash the cockles thoroughly in plenty of cold water — if there is time leave them to soak for a couple of hours.

Bring a saucepan of water to the boil and put the cockles into this for a few minutes, until the shells have opened.

Strain, and when cool pick the cockles out of the shells.

Fry the streaky bacon until crisp.

Lift out of the frying pan and keep warm.

Toss the cockles in the bacon fat until they are lightly browned.

Serve the cockles and bacon on hot, buttered toast.

POTTED SHRIMPS

Before the advent of the deep freeze, 'potting' was an important method of preserving meat and fish. The spices and the seal of clarified butter were the chief preserving agents. Prawns, lobsters, crabs or crayfish may also be prepared in the following way.

1 lb (450 g) shelled shrimps (or other shellfish)
8 oz (225 g) butter
1 teaspoon mace
½ teaspoon powdered ginger
A pinch of salt
A pinch of cayenne pepper

Finely chop half the shrimps and leave the other half whole.

Melt 6 oz (175 g) of the butter and stir in the shrimps.

Add the mace, ginger, salt and cayenne pepper.

Stir over a low heat until all the butter is absorbed into the mixture.

Spoon the mixture into small jars or moulds.

While still hot, melt the rest of the butter and pour over the top.

Leave overnight to cool.

Turn out to serve, with hot toast.

ROAST GOOSE

Before the turkey became so popular, goose used to be the traditional festive meal in England. It is said that Queen Elizabeth I received news of the English victory over the Spanish Armada while eating roast goose on Michaelmas Day. She therefore ordained that this was to be the traditional meal for Michaelmas. Coming at the end of the harvest, it was fattened on gleanings left by the harvesters, and was often stuffed with rabbit joints.

Geese were important not just for their meat, but for the down and feathers, and for their fat. Goose grease had many uses — it was eaten as a spread on bread, used as a poultice for bad chests; rubbed on hands to prevent chapping in cold weather; and smeared on to leather harness to keep it supple.

Roast goose is traditionally stuffed with sage and onion, or with prunes and apple. Calculate the cooking time at about 15 minutes per lb (450 g) — but really large birds take less.

To roast a goose:

Stuff the goose with your chosen stuffing.

Place it on a rack in a roasting tin.

Rub salt into the skin.

Pour over a glass of wine and about ½ pint (300 ml/ 1¼ cups) stock made from the giblets.

Put into a hot oven for 20 minutes, then reduce the temperature for the rest of the roasting time.

Baste with the juices two or three times during the roasting.

20 minutes before the end of the cooking time put the goose into a clean roasting tin and raise the temperature so that the skin will become crisp.

From the first roasting tin pour off as much fat as possible and use the meaty juices to make gravy — if you put the stock into a flat bowl and leave it in the fridge the fat should solidify and make this task much easier.

Oven: 425°F/220°C Gas Mark 7
Reduce to: 350°F/180°C Gas Mark 4

ROAST TURKEY

Norfolk has long been a centre of poultry rearing. Daniel Defoe, travelling around England in the 18th century, wrote of the huge flocks of turkey and geese being driven to London markets. The Norfolk black turkey, which can still be found in some parts, does not have the plump breast of the white ones, and is more elongated in appearance.

1 turkey
1 lb (450 g) sausage meat (optional)
3 rashers streaky bacon

For the stuffing:
8 oz (225 g) fresh white breadcrumbs
2 tablespoons chopped parsley
1 tablespoon chopped thyme
Finely grated rind of 1 lemon
Salt and pepper
4 oz (100 g) softened butter
2 egg yolks

To make the stuffing:

Mix together the breadcrumbs, herbs and lemon rind.

Season with salt and pepper.

Beat the egg yolks into the softened butter and add to breadcrumb mixture.

Stuff the crop of the turkey with this mixture — and, if liked, put seasoned sausage meat inside the body.

Truss the turkey and place in a roasting tray.

Lay the bacon rashers over the breast.

Roast in a hot oven for 20 minutes, then reduce the temperature — allow 15 minutes cooking time per lb (450 g).

About 20 minutes before the end of cooking time remove the bacon to allow the breast to brown.

Remove the trussing string before serving.

Serve with gravy and cranberry sauce.

Oven: 425°C/220°F Gas Mark 7
Reduce to: 350°C/180°C Gas Mark 4

AN OLD NORFOLK STUFFING RECIPE

This is sufficient for a large turkey.

2 onions
2 oz (50 g) ham
8 oz (225 g) fresh white breadcrumbs
8 oz (225 g) shredded suet
1 tablespoon chopped parsley
A pinch of nutmeg
A pinch of marjoram
Salt and pepper
Juice and grated rind of 1 lemon
4 eggs

Chop the onions and ham finely.

Mix together the chopped onions and ham, breadcrumbs, shredded suet, parsley, nutmeg, marjoram, lemon juice and rind.

Season with salt and pepper.

Bind together with the lightly beaten eggs.

A HEN ON HER NEST

When this dish was eaten by farming families in the 19th century, the hard-boiled eggs were served to the children and the adults ate the chicken.

1 boiling fowl, weighing about 3 lbs (1.5 kg)
2 carrots
2 medium onions
6 peppercorns
½ teaspoon ground ginger
½ teaspoon mace
A pinch of salt
A sprig each of parsley and thyme
2 oz (50 g) butter
4 eggs
8 oz (225 g) rice
1 oz (25 g) flour
¼ pint (150 ml/ ⅔ cup) milk
4 tablespoons (⅓ cup) double cream

Put the chicken, chopped carrots and onions, peppercorns, ginger, mace, salt, and chopped herbs in a saucepan and cover with water.

Bring to the boil and simmer for 2 hours.

Lift out the chicken and place in a roasting tin, and reserve the stock.

Dot the top of the chicken with 1 oz (25 g) of the butter.

Cook in a moderate oven for 10 minutes until it is nicely browned, then keep warm.

Hard-boil the eggs.

Cook the rice in 1 pint (600 ml/ 2½ cups) of the chicken stock.

Melt the remaining 1 oz (25 g) of butter in a saucepan and stir in the flour.

Cook gently for 2 minutes, then stir in ½ pint (300 ml/ 1¼ cups) of the stock and the milk.

Simmer until the sauce thickens, then add the cream and season well.

Put the hard-boiled eggs in the centre of a large serving dish and arrange the rice around the edges.

Pour half the sauce over the eggs.

Put the chicken on top of the eggs and serve.

The rest of the sauce may be handed separately.

Oven: 350°F/180°C Gas Mark 4

Hen & Chickens

PHEASANT CASSEROLE

Serves 6

A brace of pheasant
2 oz (50 g) butter
8 oz (225 g) small onions
8 oz (225 g) button mushrooms
1 oz (25 g) plain flour
1 pint (600 ml/ 2½ cups) stock
1 glass of red wine
Grated rind and juice of 1 orange
1 tablespoon redcurrant jelly
1 tablespoon chopped parsley
Salt and pepper

Cut the pheasant into pieces.

Melt the butter in a frying pan and brown the pheasant pieces.

Remove them to a casserole.

Add the onions and mushrooms to the frying pan and cook gently for a few minutes.

Remove them to the casserole and stir the flour into the remaining butter in the frying pan.

Gradually add the stock, stirring until the sauce thickens.

Add the wine, rind and juice of the orange, redcurrant jelly and parsley.

Season to taste.

Pour the sauce over the pheasant and vegetables in the casserole dish.

Cover and cook in a moderate oven or 1½-2 hours, until the pheasant is tender.

Oven: 325°F/160°C Gas Mark 3

PIGEON PIE

This pie was traditionally served on 14th May, the day the maids started their holiday.

4 pigeons
12 oz (350 g) braising steak
Seasoned flour
1 oz (25 g) lard or butter
¾ pint (450 ml/ 2 cups) water
2 hard-boiled eggs
½ oz (15 g) gelatine
1 onion
A spig each of parsley and thyme
8 oz (225 g) puff pastry

Joint the pigeons and cut the steak into cubes.

Toss in the seasoned flour.

Melt the lard in a saucepan and fry all the meat until golden brown.

Add the water and bring to the boil.

Cover and simmer for about 1½ hours, until the meat is tender.

Lift out the meat with a perforated spoon and transfer it to a pie dish.

Remove the bones from the pigeon joints.

Put the hard-boiled eggs into the meat mixture.

Dissolve the gelatine in a little water over a bowl of hot water.

Pour in a thin stream into the reserved stock, stirring all the time.

Add the chopped onion and herbs.

PARTRIDGE STEW

The grain fields in Norfolk attract vast numbers of partridge and pheasants. Great shooting parties were held on the Norfolk estates.

A brace of partridge
2 oz (50 g) butter
4 slices ham
2 tomatoes
4 oz (100 g) button mushrooms
1 clove of garlic
4 cloves
6 peppercorns
Salt
A pinch of thyme
1½ pints (900 ml/ 3¾ cups) stock
A glass of port or red wine

Cut the birds into halves.

Melt the butter in a large saucepan and brown the pieces of meat.

Add the ham cut in strips, the skinned tomatoes, mushrooms, garlic, cloves, peppercorns, salt and thyme.

Cover with the stock, and add a glass of port or red wine.

Bring to the boil and simmer slowly for about 2 hours.

Lift the meat out on to a serving dish.

Skim any fat from the top of the stock.

Mix one tablespoon cornflour with a little water and add to the stock in the saucepan to thicken.

Pour the gravy over the partridge pieces and garnish the dish with triangles of toast.

Pour the stock over the meat in the pie dish.

Leave to cool.

Roll out the pastry to make a lid.

Make a hole in the top, and brush with milk or beaten egg to glaze.

Bake in a hot oven for about 30 minutes, until the pastry is well risen and golden brown.

Serve cold.

Oven: 425°F/220°C Gas Mark 7

GRILLED PARTRIDGE   Serves 4

2 partridge
1 tablespoon flour
Salt
Cayenne pepper
Butter

Spilt the partridge in halves.

Mix together the flour, and a little salt and cayenne pepper.

Sprinkle over the partridge halves.

Cook under a hot grill, insides first.

Brush with a little melted butter before serving.

GAME PIE

1 lb (450 g) cold cooked game — pheasant, partridge, woodpigeon, etc.
8 rashers streaky bacon
4 hard-boiled eggs
1 tablespoon chopped parsley
2 oz (50 g) butter
8 oz (225 g) mushrooms
1 large onion
1 oz (25 g) flour
½ pint (300 ml/ 1¼ cups) stock from boiling the game birds
Salt and pepper
8 oz (225 g) puff or shortcrust pastry

Put the game birds into a large pan with a bouquet garni.

Cover with water, bring to the boil and simmer until the meat falls away from the bone.

Arrange the meat in a pie dish.

Reserve the stock.

Remove the rind from the bacon rashers and lay them over the meat.

Slice the hard-boiled eggs and put in a layer on top of the bacon.

Sprinkle over the chopped parsley.

Melt the butter in a saucepan and gently cook the sliced onion and mushrooms until they are soft and golden brown.

Stir in the flour and cook for another couple of minutes.

Gradually stir in ½ pint (300 ml/ 1¼ cups) of the reserved stock.

Bring to the boil and simmer gently for a couple of minutes.

Season well with salt and pepper.

Pour the sauce over the meat in the pie dish — it should come to about ½ inch (1 cm) from the top.

Roll out the pastry to make a lid.

Brush with beaten egg to glaze.

Bake in a hot oven for about 35-40 minutes, or until the pastry is golden brown.

Oven: 425°F/220°C Gas Mark 7

FRIED GUINEA FOWL

Serves 4

1 guinea fowl
Salt and pepper
2 oz (50 g) butter
1 onion
2 rashers streaky bacon
4 oz (100 g) button mushrooms
1 oz (25 g) flour
¼ pint (150 ml/ ⅔ cup) stock
¼ pint (150 ml/ ⅔ cup) white wine

Joint the guinea fowl into four pieces and season with salt and pepper.

Melt half the butter in a large pan and brown the joints.

Cover the pan and cook gently for about 30 minutes, until the flesh is tender.

Remove the joints to a serving dish and keep warm.

Add more butter to the pan and fry the chopped onion, bacon and mushrooms.

Sprinkle over the flour, stir and cook for a couple of minutes.

Stir in the stock and wine and bring to the boil so that the sauce thickens.

Adjust the seasoning, pour the sauce over the joints, and serve.

STUFFED GUINEA FOWL

Serves 4

The celery and watercress 'stuffing' in this recipe is used for flavouring only — it is not eaten as part of the dish.

2 small guinea fowl
1 stick of celery
3 sprigs of watercress
1 clove of garlic
Salt and pepper
3 oz (75 g) butter
1 lemon
A glass of dry white wine
½ pint (300 ml/ 1¼ cups) stock
2 egg yolks

Chop the celery and watercress, crush the garlic, and bind them all together with 1 oz (25 g) of the butter.

Season with salt and pepper and put into the birds.

Mix the grated rind from the lemon with salt and pepper and rub over the skin of the guinea fowl.

Melt 2 oz (50 g) of the butter in a large pan and brown the birds.

Pour in the wine and stock and bring to the boil.

Cover and simmer for about 45 minutes.

Lift out the guinea fowl, drain, and remove the stuffing.

Joint each bird into halves, put on a serving dish and keep warm.

Beat the juice from the lemon and the egg yolks together.

Add a little of the hot stock, then pour into the pan.

Heat through gently without boiling until the sauce thickens.

Pour the sauce over the joints and garnish with lemon slices.

WILD DUCK

The Norfolk Broads are home to various kinds of wild duck — mallard, shovellers, and pochards — and to greylag geese. They are in season from the beginning of September to the end of February. Here is one way of roasting them.

Wild duck
Butter
Orange juice

For the sauce:
1 tablespoon lemon juice
1 tablespoon sugar
2 tablespoons port
1 tablespoon tomato ketchup
Salt
Cayenne pepper

Place the duck in a roasting tin.

Put a knob of butter inside each, and pour over some orange juice.

Roast in a moderately hot oven for about 30 minutes, or until tender, basting occasionally with the orange juice.

Mix all the sauce ingredients together and pour over the duck before serving.

Oven: 375°F/190°C Gas Mark 5

RABBIT HOT POT

Rabbit, freely available, formed a major part of the farmworkers' diet.

1 rabbit
1 oz (25 g) flour
Salt and pepper
Grated nutmeg
1 oz (25 g) butter
4 oz (100 g) fresh white breadcrumbs
2 rashers bacon
Grated rind of 1 lemon

Grease an ovenproof dish or casserole.

Prepare and joint the rabbit.

Season the flour with salt, pepper and grated nutmeg and dust the rabbit joints with it.

Fry the joints in the butter until golden brown.

Put half the breadcrumbs in the bottom of the casserole, then half the rabbit, and the two rashers of bacon.

Add the rest of the breadcrumbs, the grated lemon rind, and finish with the other half of the rabbit.

Half fill the casserole with water, cover, and cook in a moderate oven for about 1 hour, or until the rabbit meat is tender.

Oven: 325°F/160°C Gas Mark 3.

AUTUMN RABBIT AND NORFOLK DUMPLINGS

Serves 4

1 rabbit
1 oz (25 g) lard
1 oz (25 g) flour
½ pint (300 ml/ 1¼ cups) ale
1 onion
1 carrot
1 large apple
2 oz (50 g) button mushrooms
A sprig each of parsley and thyme
1 bay leaf
Salt and pepper

Cut the rabbit into joints and brown them in the melted lard.

Remove the joints to a casserole dish.

Stir the flour into the hot fat, cook for a couple of minutes, then add the ale, stirring until the sauce thickens.

Pour the sauce over the rabbit joints in the casserole.

Peel and slice the onion, carrot and apple and add to the casserole.

Chop the mushrooms and herbs and add them, with the bay leaf, to the casserole.

Season with salt and pepper.

Cover and cook in a moderate oven for about 2 hours, until the rabbit joints are tender.

Put the Norfolk Dumplings (see recipe) on top of the casserole for the last 20 minutes of cooking time.

Remove the bay leaf before serving.

Oven: 350°F/180°C Gas Mark 4.

RABBIT PIE

1 rabbit
1 small onion
Salt and pepper
4 hard-boiled eggs
8 oz (225 g) puff pastry

Prepare and joint the rabbit.

Put the rabbit joints and sliced onion into a saucepan and cover with water.

Season with salt and pepper.

Bring to the boil, cover, and simmer for 1-1½ hours, until the meat is tender.

Lift out the rabbit joints with a perforated spoon and leave to cool.

Reserve the stock.

Remove the meat from the bones and put into a pie dish.

Add the hard-boiled eggs to the rabbit meat.

Pour over enough of the reserved stock to come halfway up the pie dish.

Roll out the pastry to cover the dish.

Make a couple of slits in the top and brush with milk or beaten egg to glaze.

Bake in a hot oven for about 30 minutes, until the pastry is well-risen and golden brown.

Oven: 425°F/220°C Gas Mark 7

ROAST RABBIT

Serves 4

1 rabbit
2 onions
4 oz (100 g) fresh white breadcrumbs
1 tablespoon chopped sage
Salt and pepper
Seasoned flour
Milk

Prepare and clean the rabbit, and leave in salted cold water for a couple of hours for the flesh to whiten.

Meanwhile make the stuffing.

Boil the onions until soft and chop into small pieces.

Mix with the breadcrumbs and sage, and season with salt and pepper to taste.

Dry the rabbit and fill with the stuffing.

Stitch up the cavity to stop the stuffing falling out during roasting.

Coat the rabbit with seasoned flour.

Place in a roasting tin and dot the top with lard.

Pour in enough milk to come halfway up the rabbit.

Roast in a moderate oven for about 1 hour, or until flesh is browned.

Thicken the milk sauce with a little flour to make gravy.

Remove the trussing string before serving.

Oven: 180°C/350°F Gas Mark 4

JUGGED HARE

Serves 6-8

Hare is in season from September to the end of February. This dish gets its
name from the deep, lidded stoneware jug in which it was traditionally cooked.

1 hare
A little flour
2 onions
6 cloves
A sprig each of parsley and thyme
6 each whole allspice and peppercorns
A strip of lemon peel
A glass of port wine

Prepare the hare and cut into small joints.

Dust the joints with flour and put into a saucepan.

Add the onions stuck with cloves, chopped herbs, allspice,
peppercorns and lemon peel.

Cover with water, bring to the boil and simmer for about 2
hours until the meat is tender.

Lift out the pieces of meat on to a serving dish.

Thicken the stock with a tablespoonful of flour mixed with
a little water.

Add the glass of port.

Boil for another five minutes, then strain through a sieve and
pour over the hare.

Serve with redcurrant jelly.

PIG'S FRY

Every country family used to keep a pig, and the autumn pig-killing was an important event. Nothing from the pig was wasted, the most perishable parts being used up first. The offal — a mixture of the liver, kidney, belly, heart and brain — was used in a dish called pig's fry. Often it was served with Norfolk dumplings — or floaters, as they are called locally.

1 lb (450 g) pig's fry
1 oz (25 g) flour seasoned with salt and pepper
1 oz (25 g) lard

Cut the fry into small pieces and coat with the seasoned flour.

Put them into a ovenproof dish or roasting tin and dot with the lard.

Bake in a moderate oven for about an hour.

Serve hot, with the pan juices.

Oven: 350°F/180°C Gas Mark 4

STUFFED CHINE

Roast pork chine with apple sauce was a popular joint in in the 18th century. The carcase of the pig used to be cut so that the chine was taken from the back of the animal between the shoulder blades. These days the carcase is cut in a different way and chine remains popular only in parts of Norfolk and in Lincolnshire. Stuffed chine is eaten cold, with vinegar to bring out the sharp flavour. You can buy it ready prepared from the butcher's, or uncooked to stuff yourself. Before the invention of aluminium foil the chine would be covered in a huff pastry of flour and water to protect it from drying out during baking.

A chine of pork

For the herb stuffing:
3-4 tablespoons chopped parsley
1 large leek, finely chopped
1 tablespoon chopped marjoram
1 teaspoon ground mace

Weigh the meat to calculate the cooking time — it will need 20 minutes per lb (450 g).

Soak the chine in cold water for at least 12 hours.

Wipe it dry.

Score the meat deeply on both sides.

Pound the stuffing ingredients together — or put them in a food processor — so that you have a moist hash.

Press the stuffing into the slashes in the meat.

Wrap the joint in aluminium foil and put into a baking tray.

Alternatively, the stuffed chine may be tied tightly into a pudding cloth and boiled, allowing 30 minutes for the first pound (450 g) and 15 minutes for each pound thereafter.

Bake in a moderate oven for the calculated time.

When cooked, remove the foil and leave the chine to cool.

Cut into slices and serve cold with vinegar and a green salad.

Oven: 350°F/180°C Gas Mark 4

PIG'S EARS WITH TARTARE SAUCE

When the pig's head was being prepared for making brawn, the ears were removed and eaten as a delicacy on their own. Every part of the ear can be eaten — the cartilage gives a contrast to the rather gelatinous meat.

2 pigs' ears
A pinch of salt
2 carrots
1 onion
6 cloves
A bouquet garni
Seasoned flour
Yolk of 1 egg
Breadcrumbs
Oil for deep-frying

Soak the ears in salted water for a few hours.

Drain and put into a saucepan.

Cover with water and add a pinch of salt.

Bring to the boil and skim before adding the sliced carrots, onion stuck with cloves, and bouquet garni.

Simmer for 1½-2 hours, until tender.

Cut the ears into strips.

Toss the strips in seasoned flour.

Coat with the egg yolk, and then the breadcrumbs.

Deep-fry in oil.

Serve with tartare sauce.

HOG'S HEAD CHEESE

This brawn was popular with the Edwardians as a breakfast dish. These days it would probably be preferred as a lunch or supper dish, with hot baked jacket potatoes and pickles.

Half a pig's head
1 dressed cow-heel
A faggot of herbs
Brown sugar

Clean the head well and soak it with the cow-heel in cold water for at least 5 hours.

Put them into a pan of fresh water.

Bring to the boil and simmer for about 3 hours, until the meat falls away from the bone.

Lift the head and cow-heel out of the pan and remove the bones.

Cut the meat into small pieces.

Strain the stock.

Put the meat and strained stock back into the saucepan with the faggot of herbs and some brown sugar according to taste.

Bring back to the boil and simmer until the stock is reduced to half the original quantity.

Remove the faggot of herbs.

Put the meat into a wetted mould.

Pour over the stock.

Leave in a cool place to set.

Serve cold, sliced, with a salad and hot jacket potatoes.

PORK PUDDING

Serves 4

1 lb shoulder of pork, minced
4 oz (100 g) raisins
A little pork fat
Salt and pepper
4 oz (100 g) plain flour
1 egg
½ pint (300 ml/ 1¼ cups) milk

Put the minced pork and raisins into an ovenproof dish.

Season with salt and pepper and dot the top with pork fat.

Bake in a moderately hot oven for half an hour.

Meanwhile sift the flour and a pinch of salt into a bowl, and make a well in the centre.

Break the egg into the well and gradually draw in the flour from the sides, beating to a thick paste.

Add the milk a little at a time, stirring to remove any lumps.

Beat the batter thoroughly until small air bubbles appear all over the surface.

Pour the batter over the meat, increase the temperature of the oven, and bake for a further 30 minutes until the batter is well-risen and brown.

Oven: 375°F/190°C Gas Mark 5
Increase to: 425°F/220°C Gas Mark 7

NORFOLK PLOUGH PUDDING

Savoury suet puddings were a variation of the traditional dumpling, consisting of meat or fish encased in the suet crust.

8 oz (225 g) self-raising flour
4 oz (100 g) shredded suet
1 lb (450 g) pork sausage meat
4 oz (100 g) streaky bacon
1 onion
1 tablespoon chopped sage
Salt and pepper

Grease a 2 pint (1.15 litre) pudding basin.

Mix together the flour and suet, a pinch of salt, and enough water to make a firm dough.

Roll out the dough and use two-thirds of it to line the pudding basin.

Mix together the sausage meat, chopped bacon, onion and sage and season with salt and pepper.

Press the meat mixture into the pudding basin.

Use the remaining pastry to make a lid.

Cover with greaseproof paper and a piece of foil.

Steam for 4 hours, or reduce the steaming time by using a pressure cooker.

Serve hot with tomato sauce.

PORK CHEESE

Pork cheese was made from the hock — the lower half of the front leg — of the pig, which was first lightly pickled in brine. It is called 'cheese' because it has similiar texture and consistency.

A hock of salt pork, with trotter
1 tablespoon finely chopped sage
Salt and pepper

Soak the hock in water overnight.

Next day put it in a saucepan covered with fresh water, bring to the boil and simmer for about 2 hours, until the meat is leaving the bone.

Cut the meat up finely, and put it into a basin or mould.

Add the chopped sage and season with salt and pepper.

Continue boiling the bones in the stock until the liquid has reduced by half.

Pour over the meat in the basin and leave in a cool place to set.

Grazier

SAUSAGE AND ONION STEW

Serves 4

4 large onions
Salt
1 lb (450 g) pork sausages
1 pint (600 ml/ 2½ cups) milk

Peel the onions and put into a large saucepan with about 2 pints (1.15 litres/ 5 cups) of salted water.

Bring to the boil, cover, and simmer for another 30 minutes.

Add the pork sausages, bring back to the boil and simmer for another 30 minutes.

Strain off half the liquid and add the milk.

Reheat but do not boil.

Serve with mashed potatoes and peas.

SALT BEEF AND DUMPLINGS

A piece of silverside, weighing about 3 lbs (1.5 kg)
6 pints (3.5 litres/ 15 cups) water
1 lb (450 g) salt — preferably sea salt
2 oz (50 g) saltpetre
8 oz (225 g) brown sugar
2 onions
2 carrots
2 bay leaves
10 black peppercorns
A sprig each of parsley and thyme

Put the meat in a large earthenware bowl or plastic tub.

Add the salt, saltpetre and sugar to the water, and pour over the meat.

Cover the bowl and leave the meat to soak for about a week.

To cook the salt beef, put it into a large saucepan with the chopped onions and carrots, bay leaves, peppercorns and chopped herbs.

Cover with water, bring to the boil and simmer for 2-2½ hours, or until the beef is tender.

Add the dumplings (see recipe) 20 minutes before the end of cooking time.

Cow

OXTAIL STEW WITH NORFOLK DUMPLINGS

Serves 4

Start preparing this dish the day before you want to eat it. The meat should be partially cooked, so that when it is cold the fat can be skimmed off. The haricot beans should be soaked overnight.

1 oxtail
8 oz (225 g) chuck steak
2 onions
Salt
4 oz (100 g) haricot beans, soaked overnight
1 lb (450 g) carrots

Wash the oxtail thoroughly in cold water and cut into pieces.

Cut the chuck steak into small cubes and slice the onions.

Put the oxtail, steak and onions into a large saucepan and cover with salted water.

Bring to the boil, cover, and simmer for 2½ hours.

Leave to cool overnight.

Next day skim all the fat from the top, and add the soaked haricot beans and sliced carrots.

Bring to the boil, cover, and simmer for 2-3 hours, until the meat is tender.

Add suet dumplings (see recipe) 20 minutes before the end of cooking time.

GIBLET PIE

2 sets of chicken giblets
1 lb (450 g) stewing beef
Seasoned flour
1 onion
A bouquet garni, or 1 teaspoon dried mixed herbs
8 oz (225 g) puff pastry

Clean the giblets.

Cut the beef into small pieces and roll in seasoned flour.

Put the giblets and beef into a saucepan with the sliced onion and bouquet garni or dried herbs.

Add enough water to cover, bring to the boil and simmer for two hours, or until the meat is tender.

Remove the meat from the pan and cut up the giblets.

Place all the meat in an ovenproof dish and cover with reserved stock.

Roll out the pastry to make a lid.

Cut a couple of slits in the top and brush with milk or beaten egg to glaze.

Bake in a hot oven for about 35 minutes, until the pastry is well-risen and golden brown.

Oven: 425°F/220° Gas Mark 7

DRESSMAKER TRIPE

Serves 4

The name of this dish reflects the fact that the tripe is sewn up at the edges to contain the stuffing.

A piece of prepared tripe, about 1-1½ lbs (450-675 g) in weight
1 large onion
4 oz (100 g) fresh white breadcrumbs
A sprig of each of parsley and thyme
Salt and pepper
4 slices streaky bacon

Boil the onion until it is soft.

Mix the boiled onion, breadcrumbs and chopped herbs together to make the stuffing.

Season with salt and pepper.

Spread the stuffing over half the piece of tripe and fold the other half on top of it.

Sew the edges of the tripe together.

Put the tripe in a greased baking tin and lay the slices of bacon on top.

Bake in a moderate oven for 1 hour.

Serve with a good brown gravy.

Oven: 350°F/180°C Gas Mark 4

LEG OF LAMB IN A SUET CRUST

Serves approx. 8

A leg of lamb

For the suet crust:
1 lb (450 g) self-raising flour
8 oz (225 g) shredded suet

(These quantities may vary according to the size of the leg of lamb.)

Wipe the leg of lamb with a clean cloth and sprinkle it with salt.

Mix the flour and shredded suet with enough water to make a firm dough.

Roll this out until it is large enough to wrap round the leg of lamb, enclosing it like a parcel.

Tie securely in a floured cloth and put into a large saucepan.

Cover with water, bring to the boil and simmer for up to 4 hours — according to the size — until the meat is tender.

When cooked take off the suet crust and serve it with the sliced lamb and gravy made from the juices.

Lamb

ASPARAGUS

Norfolk asparagus has fat green stalks, and is in season from May to early July.

1 lb (450 g) asparagus
1 oz (25 g) butter
1 teaspoon caster sugar
Salt and pepper

Cook the asparagus in a pan of salted water for about 5-6 minutes.

Drain well.

Melt the butter and fry the asparagus gently for 5 minutes.

Sprinkle over the sugar, and season with salt and pepper.

SAMPHIRE

This plant grows wild in the sandhills around Snettisham. It is gathered during July and August and can be eaten like asparagus, boiled and served with melted butter. Traditionally it was pickled to last through the winter. It is sometimes known as 'Poor Man's Asparagus'.

MILLION PIE

Million is the old word for marrow, which used to be considered a fruit, rather than a vegetable.

8 oz (225 g) shortcrust pastry
2 oz (50 g) jam
1 lb (450 g) vegetable marrow
1 egg
A pinch of ground nutmeg
1 oz (25 g) sugar

Roll out the pastry and line a greased 7 inch (18 cm) flan tin.

Reserve the pastry trimmings to decorate the top of the pie.

Spread the pastry base with the jam.

Peel and seed the marrow and cut into slices.

Put into a saucepan, cover with water and boil until soft.

Drain well to remove all the liquid.

Leave to cool.

With a fork, beat the cooled marrow and eggs together.

Add the nutmeg and the sugar.

Spoon the mixture into the pastry case.

Sprinkle a little more nutmeg on top.

Cut the left-over pastry into strips to decorate the top.

Bake in a hot oven for 10 minutes, then reduce the temperature to moderate and bake for a further 20 minutes, until the pastry is golden brown.

Oven: 425°F/220°C Gas Mark 7
Reduce to: 350°F/180°C Gas Mark 4

APPLE PIE

Serves 6

12 oz (350 g) shortcrust pastry
2 lbs (900 g) cooking apples
A knob of butter
1 oz (25 g) sugar
2 tablespoons marmalade
1 oz (25 g) currants

Roll out half the pastry to line an 8 inch (20 cm) pie plate.

Peel, core and slice the apples.

Melt the butter in a pan and add the apples, cooking them gently without water until reduced to a pulp.

Stir in the sugar and leave to cool.

Put half the apple pulp into the pastry case, followed by the marmalade and the currants, and then the remaining apple pulp.

Roll out the rest of the pastry to make a lid.

Damp, seal and trim the edges.

Make a couple of slits in the top to allow the steam to escape.

Bake in a moderate oven for 15 minutes, then reduce the temperature and bake for a further 25-30 minutes.

Oven: 425°F/220°C Gas Mark 7
Reduce to: 350°F/180°C Gas Mark 4

FRITTER PIE

After the autumn pig-killing, surplus pig fat was rendered down over a low heat until all the fat had melted. The lard was used for cooking, and the left-over scratchings, or fritters, made Fritter Pie.

12 oz (350 g) shortcrust pastry
Fritters
2 large cooking apples
2 oz (50 g) sultanas
1 oz (25 g) brown sugar
1 level teaspoon mixed spice
1 oz (15 g) granulated sugar

Roll out half the pastry to line a greased pie plate.

Peel, core and slice the apples and mix with the fritters, sultanas, brown sugar and the mixed spice to fill the pastry base.

Roll out the remaining pastry to make a lid.

Seal and trim the edges.

Dissolve the granulated sugar in a little water to make a syrup and brush the top of the pie to glaze.

Bake in a moderately hot oven for 30-40 minutes, until the pastry is golden brown.

Oven: 400°F/200°C Gas Mark 6

TOFFEE APPLE PUDDING

Serves 6

This delicious pudding will turn out, when cooked, covered with a rich toffee sauce.

8 oz (225 g) plain flour
6 oz (175 g) shredded suet
2 oz (50 g) softened butter
2 oz (50 g) brown sugar
1½ lb (675 g) cooking apples

Mix the flour and shredded suet with enough water to make a firm dough.

Roll out ⅔ of the dough on a floured surface, reserving the remainder for the lid.

Cream the softened butter and brown sugar together and spread liberally all round a pie dish.

Line the dish with the suet crust pastry.

Peel, core and slice the apples.

Put into the pastry-lined pie dish.

Roll out the remaining pastry to make a lid.

Dampen the edges of the pastry and press firmly together to seal.

Bake in a moderate oven for 1¼ hours.

Oven: 350°F/180°C Gas Mark 4

NORFOLK PUDDING

Use apples that keep their shape well for this pudding — cooking apples
disintegrate too quickly.

4 oz (100 g) plain flour
A pinch of salt
1 egg
½ pint (300 ml/ 1¼ cups) milk
1 lb (450 g) apples
A knob of lard
2 oz (50 g) sugar
2 oz (50 g) currants

Sift the flour and salt into a mixing basin and make a well
in the centre.

Break the egg into the well and gradually add the milk,
bringing in the flour from the sides.

Beat well until the batter is smooth and free from lumps.

Peel, core and slice the apples thinly.

Put the slices into an ovenproof dish with the knob of lard
and bake in a hot oven for 5 minutes.

Remove the dish from the oven, sprinkle on the sugar and
currants, and pour over the batter.

Return the dish to the oven and bake for a further 30 minutes.

Serve hot, sprinkled with sugar.

Oven: 425°F/220°C Gas Mark 7

APPLE PUDDING

Serves 4

1½ lb (675 g) cooking apples
8 oz (225 g) self-raising flour
6 oz (175 g) shredded suet
3 oz (75 g) soft brown sugar
2 oz (50 g) butter

Peel, core and slice the apples.

Mix the flour and shredded suet with enough water to make a dough.

Soften the butter and cream together with 2 oz (50 g) of the brown sugar.

Spread this creamed mixture all over the bottom and sides of a 1½ pint (900 ml) pudding basin.

Roll out ¾ of the suet pastry and line the pudding basin.

Put in the prepared apple and sprinkle with the remaining 1 oz (25 g) sugar.

Roll out the remaining pastry to make a lid.

Cover with greaseproof paper and a pudding cloth, or aluminium foil.

Place in a saucepan of boiling water, cover tightly and steam for 3-3½ hours — or use a pressure cooker to reduce the steaming time.

When cooked, turn out on to a serving dish — the pudding will be covered in a rich, toffee-like sauce.

BLACK CAPS

Serves 4

A local variety of hard sweet apple called Beefing, or Biffin is used in this recipe. The apples used to be packed down in layers and slowly dried in the bread ovens after baking to produce the round wrinkled fruit used in this recipe.

4 beefings
Rind of ½ lemon, thinly peeled and sliced
1 oz (25 g) chopped mixed peel
4 oz (100 g) soft brown sugar
A glass of red wine

Cut the apples in half vertically and scoop out the cores.

Fill them with the lemon rind and mixed peel, put the halves together again and pack them into an ovenproof dish.

Spoon the sugar into the spaces inbetween.

Pour over the glass of wine.

Bake in a hot oven for 10-15 minutes until the apples turn dark brown.

Then cover with foil, reduce the temperature and continue baking until the apples are soft.

Oven: 450°F/230°C Gas Mark 8
Reduce to: 350°F/180°C Gas Mark 4

BAKED APPLE DUMPLINGS

This was a favourite dessert for luncheon at the great shooting parties held on the Norfolk estates.

12 oz (350 g) puff or shortcrust pastry
4 apples
2 oz (50 g) sugar
2 oz (50 g) sultanas
Grated nutmeg

Divide the pastry into four pieces and roll each into a square large enough to wrap over an apple.

Peel and core the apples and set in the centre of the pastry squares.

Fill each core hole with sultanas, sugar, and a pinch of nutmeg.

Gather the pasty over the tops, brushing the edges with milk to seal.

Set the apples on a floured baking tray.

Bake in a moderately hot oven for 10 minutes, then reduce the temperature and cook for a further 20 minutes.

Serve hot or cold, with cream.

Oven: 400°F/200°C Gas Mark 6
Reduce to: 300°F/150°C Gas Mark 2

TREACLE CUSTARD TART

Serves 4-6

6 oz (175 g) shortcrust pastry
4 tablespoons golden syrup
Grated rind of 1 lemon
½ oz (15 g) butter
1 egg
2 tablespoons cream

Grease an 8 inch (20 cm) sandwich tin or pie plate and line with the pastry.

Prick the base and leave to rest.

Meanwhile, heat the golden syrup gently in a saucepan and stir in the lemon rind.

Cut the butter into small pieces and stir into the syrup.

Beat the egg and cream together and stir into the the syrup.

Spoon this filling into the pastry base.

Bake in a moderate oven for about 30 minutes until set.

Serve hot or cold.

Oven: 375°F/190°C Gas Mark 5

NORWICH TART

6 oz (175 g) shortcrust pastry
2 oz (50 g) butter
4 oz (100 g) icing sugar
3 oz (75 g) ground almonds
Grated rind and juice of 1 lemon
Walnut halves and glacé cherries to decorate

Roll out the pastry and line an 8 inch (20 cm) flan tin.

Bake the pastry case blind, pricking it lightly all over, covering with greaseproof paper and filling with rice or beans to prevent it losing its shape during baking.

Bake in a hot oven for 15 minutes.

Remove the rice and the paper.

Cream together the butter and icing sugar.

Work in the ground almonds and the lemon rind and juice.

Spread the mixture into the pastry case.

Decorate the top with walnut halves and glacé cherries.

Bake in moderate oven for 25 minutes.

Oven: 425°F/220°C Gas Mark 7
Reduce to: 350°F/180°C Gas Mark 4

BREAD PUDDING

Serves 4

8 oz (225 g) stale bread
4 oz (100 g) shredded suet
4 oz (100 g) currants
2 oz (50 g) soft brown sugar
Grated rind of 1 lemon
½ teaspoon ground nutmeg
2 oz (50 g) butter

Soak the bread in water until it is soft.

Squeeze out any excess water and mix together with the shredded suet, currants, sugar, lemon rind and nutmeg.

Put the mixture into a greased ovenproof dish and dot the top with butter.

Bake in a moderately hot oven for 1 hour.

Oven: 375°F/190°C Gas Mark 5

SUMMER PUDDING

Any of the soft fruits grown in Norfolk can be used for this pudding. Make it the day before you want to eat it so that the flavours develop.

2 lbs (900 g) soft fruit — a mixture of raspberries, redcurrants, loganberries, etc.
4 oz (100 g) sugar
8 slices stale white bread

Prepare the fruit and put it into a saucepan with the sugar.

Heat gently until the sugar has dissolved and the juices have begun to run.

Remove the crusts from the slices of bread and line a 2 pint (1.15 litre) pudding basin with them, keeping two slices for the top.

Spoon in the fruit filling.

Cover with remaining slices of bread.

Put a plate on top held down by a weight.

Leave to stand overnight in a cool place.

Turn out on to a plate to serve, sliced, with cream.

STRAWBERRY AND RASPBERRY FOOL

Serves 8

1 pint (600 ml/ 2½ cups) ripe stawberries
1 pint (600 ml/ 2½ cups) raspberries
8 oz (225 g) caster sugar
1 tablespoon orange-flower water (A little fresh orange
**   juice would do)**
1½ pints (900 ml/ 3¾ cups) cream
Strawberries for decoration

Bruise the strawberries and raspberries and pass them through a sieve.

Mix in the sugar and orange-flower water.

Boil the cream and stir it until it is cold.

Beat the fruit pulp and the cold cream together until they are well mixed.

Spoon the fool into individual glasses and decorate with whole strawberries.

Fruit

PEARS IN SYRUP

This delicious dessert dish dates from medieval times.

4 cooking pears
Red wine
2 oz (50 g) sugar
1 cinnamon stick
A pinch of ground cinnamon

Peel, core and halve the pears.

Put them in a single layer in a large saucepan.

Pour over enough red wine to cover them.

Add the sugar, the cinnamon stick and the cinnamon.

Bring to the boil, cover, and simmer gently until the pears are soft.

Lift the pear halves from the pan with a perforated spoon.

Arrange them in a serving dish.

Continue boiling the liquid until it has reduced down to a syrupy consistency.

While still boiling, pour the syrup over the pears in the serving dish.

Leave to cool.

Serve cold, with cream.

CROMER CREAM

'Cream' was the name given to dessert dishes made with milk — the forerunners of today's custards and fools.

1 pint (600 ml/ 2½ cups) milk
8 oz (225 g) loaf sugar
Grated rind and juice of 1 lemon
½ oz (15 g) isinglass
2 eggs, beaten

Put the milk, sugar, lemon rind and isinglass into a saucepan.

Boil for 5 minutes.

Pour on to the beaten eggs and stir thoroughly.

Leave to cool.

When nearly cold add the lemon juice.

Pour the cream into a mould and leave in a cool place to set.

Turn out on to a plate before serving.

Lemons

SYLLABUS

Originally syllabub was made by squirting milk from the cow into some wine, cider or beer so that it made a frothy cream.

6 tablespoons (½ cup) white wine
1 tablespoon sherry
2 tablespoons brandy
1 lemon
2 oz (50 g) caster sugar
½ pint (300 ml/ 1¼ cups) double cream

Put the wine, sherry and brandy into a basin.

Peel the lemon very thinly and squeeze out the juice.

Add the peel and juice to the basin.

Leave overnight, then remove the peel.

Stir in the sugar until it dissolves.

Add the cream and whip until the mixture stands in peaks.

Put into tall glasses to serve.

Milking the Cow

FLUMMERY

Flummery is a creamy white jelly with a delicate flavour. It developed from a medieval confection called lechemeat, which was made from calves' foot broth and milk of almonds. When cooled and set this was cut into leaches (slices) and eaten with a wine sauce. Lechemeat became a cream flavoured with spices and rose-water and mixed with almonds, and isinglass was substituted for calves' foot jelly. The 'white leach' became known as flummery in the 18th century. Flummery was eaten as a second course with cream or wine poured over it. For special occasions it was made in fish-shaped moulds.

This modern version uses gelatine as a setting agent. Serve with fresh raspberries, strawberries, or whatever soft fruit is in season.

1 pint (600 ml/ 2½ cups) cream
2 oz (50 g) caster sugar
2 oz (50 g) ground almonds
½ teaspoon almond essence
Pared peel from half a lemon
A stick of cinnamon
½ oz (15 g) gelatine
3 tablespoons cold water
Flaked almonds for decoration

Put the cream, sugar, almonds and almond essence, lemon peel, and cinnamon into a saucepan.

Heat gently until the sugar has dissolved and the cream is just boiling.

Leave to cool.

Put the gelatine into a cup or small bowl and add the cold water.

Set the cup in a saucepan of simmering water until the gelatine has dissolved.

Pour the dissolved gelatine into the cream mixture, blending thoroughly.

Pour into a wetted mould.

Cover and leave in the refrigerator overnight to set.

Turn out on to a serving plate and decorate with flaked almonds.

Arrange fresh fruit around the jelly to make an attractive dessert dish.

CURD CHEESE

Curd cheese ideally needs to be made in the summer months, while the weather is warm enough to dry the curd properly.

**6 pints (3.5 litres/ 15 cups) fresh warm milk, straight
  from the cow
½ teaspoon cheese rennet**

Put the warm milk into an enamel bowl.

Add the rennet to half an eggcupful of water and tip this into the milk.

Draw a spoon through the milk a few times, then leave to set until the curd forms.

Scald a square of muslin and spread it over another bowl.

Gently tip the curd into the muslin, and gathering the corners tie string tightly round the muslin to make a secure bag.

Hang the bag up so that the whey can drip through into a bowl placed below.

Leave for about 24 hours until all the whey has drained off.

Add salt to the curd according to taste.

Line a mould with a piece of wetted muslin and ladle the curd into this, pressing it well down.

Fold the muslin over the curd and put a saucer or small plate on top, with a weight.

Change the muslin cloth each day, and after about three days the curd should be dry enough to put on a plate to dry off.

Turn the cheese every day until it has dried and a rind has formed.

HOT CROSS BUNS

Makes 20-24

According to old Norfolk folklore, Hot Cross Buns (or special bread baked on Good Friday), should be kept in a box suspended from the ceiling, or in a dry cupboard, where it would not grow mouldy like ordinary bread. A piece of bun mixed with brandy or milk would then be given to anyone suffering with dysentery or stomach trouble.

½ oz (15 g) fresh yeast
2 oz (50 g) sugar
¼ pint (150 ml/ ⅔ cup) warm milk
2 eggs
1 lb (450 g) plain flour
3 oz (75 g) butter

Cream the yeast with a little sugar and milk.

Beat the eggs and add to the creamed yeast.

Cover, and leave to rise.

Add the rest of the sugar and 3 oz (75 g) flour to the yeast mixture, and leave to rise again.

Rub the butter into the rest of the flour, add the warmed milk, and then the yeast mixture when it has risen and fallen again.

Mix to a dough and knead thoroughly.

Divide the dough into 20-24 small buns and place on greased baking sheets.

Mark a cross on the top of each, or make a cross with strips of pastry.

Brush with beaten egg or milk to glaze, and sprinkle with sugar.

Bake in a hot oven for 15-20 minutes, until well risen and golden brown.

Oven: 425°F/220°C Gas Mark 7

NORFOLK SCONE

Serves 8

1 lb (450 g) self-raising flour
1 level teaspoon salt
4 oz (100 g) butter or margarine
2 eggs
Approximately ¼ pint (150 ml/ ⅔ cup) milk

For the filling:
1 oz (25 g) butter
4 oz (100 g) currants
4 oz (100 g) demerara sugar
½ teaspoon grated nutmeg

Sift the flour and salt into a mixing basin.

Cut the butter into small pieces and rub into the flour until the mixture resembles fine breadcrumbs.

Add the beaten eggs and enough milk to make a soft dough.

Turn on to a floured board and knead lightly.

Divide the dough in half and roll out each half into an 8 inch (20 cm) round.

Put one round on to a greased baking sheet.

Spread the top with the softened butter.

Mix the currants, sugar and nutmeg together and sprinkle over the butter.

Place the second round on top.

Mark into eight wedges, half cut through.

Brush with milk to glaze, and sprinkle with a little sugar.

Bake in a hot oven for 45-50 minutes, until golden brown.

Oven: 400°F/200°C Gas Mark 6

NORFOLK SHORTCAKES

8 oz (225 g) plain flour
¼ teaspoon baking powder
4 oz (100 g) lard
2 oz (50 g) sugar
2 oz (50 g) currants

Sift the flour and baking powder into a mixing basin.

Rub in half the lard.

Add enough cold water to make a firm paste, and roll out to ½ inch (1 cm) thick.

Divide the remaining lard, the sugar and the currants into thirds.

Sprinkle one third of each over the paste, and fold into three.

Roll out again and repeat the process two more times.

Cut out into rounds or squares and place on greased baking sheets.

Bake in a moderately hot oven for about 15 minutes, until golden brown.

Dredge with caster sugar before eating.

Oven: 400°F/200°C Gas Mark 6

YARMOUTH BISCUITS

12 oz (350 g) flour
6 oz (175 g) currants
8 oz (225 g) softened butter
8 oz (225 g) sugar
3 eggs

Grease two baking sheets.

Toss the currants in a little of the flour.

Mix together the floured currants, the softened butter, sugar, flour and beaten eggs to make a thick paste.

Roll out on a floured surface and cut into rounds.

Place on the greased baking sheets and bake in a moderately hot oven for 15-20 minutes, or until golden brown.

Oven: 375°F/190°C Gas Mark 5

FAIR BUTTONS

Makes 20-24

These small biscuits were sold at the Easter Fairs held in Norwich and Great Yarmouth.

8 oz (225 g) plain flour
½ oz (15 g) ground ginger
A pinch of bicarbonate of soda
2 oz (50 g) butter
4 oz (100 g) soft dark brown sugar
4 oz (100 g) golden syrup
Grated rind of 1 lemon

Sift the flour, ginger and bicarbonate of soda into a mixing basin.

Cut the butter into small pieces and rub into the flour.

Add the sugar, golden syrup and grated lemon rind and mix thoroughly.

Roll out thinly and cut into small rounds.

Place on greased baking sheets and bake in a moderate oven for 10-12 minutes.

Lift off with a palette knife and cool on a wire tray.

Oven: 350°F/180°C Gas Mark 4

NORFOLK RUSKS

Makes about 16

These rusks used to be eaten for breakfast, spread with butter.

8 oz (225 g) self-raising flour
A pinch of salt
3 oz (75 g) butter
Milk

Sift the flour and salt into a mixing basin.

Cut the butter into small pieces and rub into the flour.

Stir in enough milk to make an elastic dough.

Roll out on a floured surface to about ¾ inch (2 cm) thick.

Cut into 1½ inch (4 cm) rounds.

Place on greased baking sheets.

Bake in a hot oven for 10 minutes.

Remove the rusks from the oven and split each one in half.

Put back on the baking sheets with the cut side upwards.

Reduce the temperature of the oven to moderate and bake for a further 15 minutes, or until the rusks are crisp and golden.

Cool and serve with butter, jam or cheese.

Oven: 425°F/220°C Gas Mark 7
Reduce to: 325°F/160°C Gas Mark 3

WEDDING CAKE

This flat currant cake was part of a traditional ceremony that took place on a wedding day. When the newly-wed couple were about to leave, the cake was broken and distributed among the unmarried girls. The girl who found a ring in her portion would shortly be married herself, and the one who found a sixpence would die an old maid.

8 oz (225 g) butter
8 oz (225 g) sugar
4 eggs
8 oz (225 g) flour
1 level teaspoon grated nutmeg
2 oz (50 g) ground almonds
8 oz (225 g) currants
4 oz (100 g) raisins
4 oz (100 g) sultanas
2 oz (50 g) cut mixed peel
3 tablespoons brandy

Grease and line a 9 inch (23 cm) cake tin.

Cream the butter and sugar together until light and fluffy.

Beat in the eggs one at a time, adding a little flour to prevent them curdling.

Fold in the sifted flour and nutmeg.

Add the dried fruit, mixed peel and brandy.

Spoon the cake mixture into the tin and bake in a moderate oven for 2-2½ hours, until firm — test with a skewer.

Oven: 325°F/160°C Gas Mark 3

NORFOLK VINEGAR CAKE

6 oz (175 g) plain flour
1 oz (25 g) cornflour
A pinch of salt
4 oz (100 g) butter
6 oz (175 g) brown sugar
2 eggs
A few drops of vanilla essence
2 tablespoons of milk
1 level teaspoon bicarbonate of soda
2 tablespoons vinegar

For the icing:
4 oz (100 g) icing sugar
1 oz (25 g) butter
1 tablespoon vinegar
½ level teaspoon mixed spice

Grease an 8 inch (20 cm) square cake tin.

Sift together the flours and salt.

Cream the butter and sugar together, adding half a tablespoon of boiling water.

Add the eggs, one at a time, with a little flour to stop them curdling.

Beat well.

Stir in the rest of the flour.

Add the vanilla essence.

Dissolve the bicarbonate of soda in the milk and then add the vinegar.

While it is still frothing stir it into the cake mixture.

Turn the mixture into the greased cake tin.

Bake in a moderately hot oven for 35-40 minutes, until firm to the touch.

Turn out on to a wire rack to cool.

To make the icing:

Put the icing sugar, butter and mixed spice into a bowl.

Boil the vinegar and beat it into the other ingredients until the icing is smooth.

Spread on top of the cooled cake.

Oven: 375°F/190°C Gas Mark 5

Acknowledgement:

Grateful thanks are extended to:
Mrs. E.A. Davy of Harleston, Norfolk, for Cromer Cream.

THE COUNTRY RECIPE SERIES

Available now @ £1.95 each

Cambridgeshire
Cornwall
Cumberland & Westmorland
Devon
Dorset
Hampshire
Kent
Lancashire
Norfolk
Somerset
Sussex
Yorkshire

Coming September 1988

Leicestershire
Oxfordshire
Suffolk
Warwickshire

All these books are available at your local bookshop or newsagent, or can be ordered direct from the publisher. Just tick the titles you require and fill in the form below. Prices and availability subject to change without notice.

Ravette Books Limited, 3 Glenside Estate, Star Road, Partridge Green, Horsham, West Sussex RH13 8RA.

Please send a cheque or postal order, and allow the following for postage and packing. UK 25p for one book and 10p for each additional book ordered.

Name ....

Address..

....

....